Two Trees

Attitudes That

Lead to Wellness

Also by Teresa Griffith

Love Your Skeletons
York Boat Captain—18 Life-Changing Days on the Peace River
Forging Sisterhood in the Frozen North

In the **Tiny Books on Big Ideas** series:
It All Belongs — The Law of Attraction and Nature of the Universe
Intelligence is Everywhere — Looking at Animals, Vegetables, and Minerals
Togetherness — Healthy Friendships, Relationships, and Communities
Tiny Books on Big Ideas, Volume 1

Two Trees

Attitudes That

Lead to Wellness

Teresa Griffith

Tiny Books on Big Ideas - Book 3

Cover design and typography by Teresa Griffith
Available for print-on-demand by Lulu.com

teresagriffith.ca

ISBN 978-0-9921204-3-6

In gratitude and appreciation

for my parents

who gave me such a great start

Contents

Acknowledgements..9

Introduction..13

Ninety Degree Turn in a Snowstorm.........17

Being in Harmony with the Universe........20

Be Willing (The Cure for Being Right).......24

Acceptance (The Cure for Frustration)......32

Complementary Colours............................36

Heart Math...46

A Sudden Impulse of Self-Destruction.......52

Gratitude (The Cure for Self-Pity).............58

Self-Acceptance...63

Trust (The Cure for Worry).........................68

Integrity (The Cure for Anxiety)................85

Remembering Stella....................................90

Humility as a Source of Joy........................96

Be Happy No Matter What (The Cure for Complaining)..103

Appendix - Chart Relating Attitudes to Chakras...111

Acknowledgements

You may have heard that writing a book is a labour of love. While it may be labour for some, for me, it is play. I am happiest when I am indulging in one of my creative outlets and I love to write, so the greater hardship would be keeping all these ideas in. It does take time, however, and many tasks such as yard work, weeding the garden and doing the dishes did suffer while I focused on finishing these tiny books. For his patience, literary suggestions, editing skill and most of all, his unbelievable love, I must thank my husband, Darren Griffith. He is so dear to me, and I know that this series would not have been as easy without his help, nor would the quality of the finished product be as high.

I must extend special thanks to all my lovely friends in Edmonton and sprinkled around Alberta. Thank you so much for all your encouragement, smiles, hugs and acceptance. I love you all!

Two friends I met when I lived up north have been invaluable in giving feedback and suggestions to the final draft. Michelle Clarke, thank you for everything. There is no doubt in my mind that these tiny books are better thanks to you. I would love to thank Tim Brown for all the deep conversations. To all my many other northern friends, I appreciate and love you more than you know!

Lastly, I must acknowledge my phenomenal family. I am who I am in large part because of the foundation you gave me. You continue to shower me with love and acceptance, along with practical help and good advice. My dad, Rudy Kneller, my mom, Donna Kneller and my sisters, Patricia and Gina, I love you and appreciate you so much.

As a being of Power, Intelligence, and Love, and the lord of his own thoughts, man holds the key to every situation, and contains within himself that transforming and regenerative agency by which he may make himself what he wills.

- James Allen in *As a Man Thinketh*

Introduction

It occurred to me that I have led a fairly unusual life. I've flown helicopters, been a volunteer fire fighter, ran a space camp, sang in a band, wrangled alpacas, and lived in tiny communities way up north. All of these activities have shaped me, which sounds like a passive statement but it is more true to say I actively did those things because of who I am. I'm not one-dimensional. I've been both shy and outgoing, quiet and talkative, meek and bold. I like travel, adventure, and thinking about why things are the way they are. I can be extroverted and introspective too, and it's my long-night ponderings that I bring you in this book.

Our attitude determines so much about our lives, yet I only recently started to think about why we have certain attitudes. How do we develop them? Do they come from our upbringing or our life experiences? Either way, that might explain why mine are so different from others—my upbringing and life experiences have been a bit unusual. Or is it possible to choose what attitudes we'd like to have? Do we control them or they us? Let's explore all these questions, along with the cures for common attitude "ailments," and what I have found to be the most beneficial attitudes for success, happiness, and bliss in life.

Your attitude is like a sand bag. If you need to hold back the rising waters, sand bags will do the trick. But there is nothing magical about the sand. If you skip the bags and just make a pile of sand to hold back water, it doesn't work. The water "melts" the sand. The sand will just end up everywhere, being washed away. The bag is all-important for making a wall that will withstand water. The bag holds the sand, giving it structure, stability, and a new purpose.

Your attitude is your outlook on life—how you consider the people around you, current events and everything else. It contains your beliefs and thoughts and gives them shape. It affects what actions you take. It helps you hold back the waters of despair, frustration, or anxiety. It's such a simple thing—like a bag—but it makes all the difference in how you experience life.

The word wellness in the title of this book refers to mental wellness. When you're mentally healthy, you can adapt to change, enjoy life, stay balanced and feel capable and energized.

I encourage you to pause after each chapter and think about what you've read. In some chapters, you may even want to pause after each paragraph. Allow the new ideas to sink in. Because these are tiny books, I often use a short way to say a big idea. Be sure to let them sink in and don't just rip through the words mindlessly. Pause, think, reread.

Two Trees

Ninety Degree Turn

in a Snowstorm

One cold, winter morning, I was driving down the highway when it started to snow. At first, there were only a few snowflakes, but as I drove, more and more of them started falling. I was headed north at first, but before long, I turned to go west.

Within minutes, the snow really started falling, and I noticed it streaming in from the right. Normally, when one drives in a snowstorm, the snow appears to come from a tunnel in front of you, but that day, the snow was definitely coming from one side. That's about the same time I noticed the wind.

There was a strong north wind blowing and howling over fields and the highway.

Soon, even more snow started falling and it began streaking across the surface of the road, driven by the wind. Now and then, I'd cross a section of highway where the snow was actually collecting—rather than bare pavement streaked with snow, it was piling up. In those areas, there were trees along the edge of the road that blocked the wind, so the snow fell onto the road and sat there.

The wind buffeted my vehicle as I drove along. For several minutes, I still noticed the snow coming from the north and every time trees sheltered the road, the wind dropped off and the snow piled up.

As I neared my destination, I turned south. The snow instantly took on the appearance of a beautiful winter wonderland. It drifted lazily down, unconcerned and unhurried. The difference between driving west and south was striking; from howling blizzard to gentle snowfall.

It is all a matter of perspective, and the

same is true in our lives. When we are looking at the world from one perspective, the wind may seem to howl and the snow pelts our face. When we turn our back to the wind, it no longer feels like a storm and the wind seems to help us. By simply turning ninety degrees and facing a different way, the world seems completely different.

We can get ourselves in a knot—anxious, frustrated, and unhappy—when we see the world as ugly, full of hateful people and we feel we have no control over what's happening. We can convince ourselves we are victims and we can get into a pattern of blaming. But a simple, ninety-degree change in attitude allows us to look at the world in a different way. We can see that we have a great deal of control over the outcomes in our lives. We see how the world is full of beauty and variety. We shift frustration into contentment, anxiety into faith and grumpiness into happiness.

Being in Harmony

with the Universe

Why are we unhappy? On one level, it is easy to answer. Whenever we obsess over our problems, get selfish, think that we have it so bad, or that life is unfair, we feel unhappy. Thoughts that focus on what we don't have lead to unhappiness in a pretty straightforward way. Could it be that gratitude is the solution to happiness?

It is almost that simple. Gratitude is the solution to self-pity, and self-pity is a very common form of unhappiness. We will explore self-pity in more detail, but it behooves us— what a great, old-fashioned word!—to get straight to the point:

The universe is all about expansion, and

we feel our discord with it (i.e. unhappy) when we forget that and try to go backwards, to contract, to hide in ourselves or in any other way resist the principle of expansion. If we stay in a moderately stable but dead-end relationship, we are unhappy because we are resisting expansion. If we focus our lives on wanting to go back to the good old days, we are resisting growth. If we tell ourselves we hate our job and would rather stay in bed, we are resisting expansion. All of these are simple examples of unhappiness caused by being resistant to all the good that is there for us to experience. It is so common to believe in all the bad in the world, it may seem very alien to believe in good, in growth and expansion, and to have faith that everything is going to work out great in the end. It's very counter-culture.

In modern western society, it is far more popular to focus on negative things and resist change. Many people fantasize about going back to some ill-defined time when life was better. In *my* fantasies, there is a place where people enjoy a gentler, less technological, less materialistic culture. People contribute instead of consuming. Everyone accepts what-is joyfully and aligns themselves with the principle of expansion. Could we learn to live in harmony with nature and with the laws of the universe?

Growth is undeniably a principle of nature. Go away for a couple of weeks in summer and see what happens to your lawn. Growth. Leave a patch of ground unplanted and see what happens. Growth—of any and every seed that lands on it. We did this one year with our garden. We live on a large acreage, and we decided to hire a young man to come with a tractor to rototill a large patch of our field. When he was done, we realized it was far too big. With no need to plant a garden on the extra area, we let it be. Within a very short time, there was every manner of weed growing there. The weeds grew like crazy—it was such good fertile soil!—and they were nearly waist-high when I finally cut them all down with a ditch mower. That's when I realized that growth—ridiculous, unhindered growth—is a principle of the Universe.

You can wish and even try to go back to the past. You can pine for the fun times of your youth, or imagine that everything was better decades ago. But you cannot go back, and following these lines of thinking will only lead to unhappiness. It's your choice, but accepting where you are and anticipating growth will help you live in harmony with the universe and be much happier overall.

Be Willing

(The Cure for Being Right)

A woman will almost happily see her husband—one she legitimately loves—struggle with lung cancer because she told him for all those years that cigarettes were going to kill him.

A middle-aged man, perfectly healthy and capable of working hard, would rather miss his truck payments and eventually have it repossessed than let go of *the need to be right* about that money someone owed him from long ago. Waiting for that money, he'll complain and sit passively on his high horse, rather than find useful work, make all his payments, and thrive.

Most of us would rather be sick, poor,

angry, or even near death than be *wrong*. Doesn't that sound crazy? Most of the population isn't crazy, is it? Somehow, we have fallen prey to a pattern of thinking in which being wrong is so horrible, we would endure anything else and consider it a moral victory as long as we are right in the end.

It is a gross distortion of pride. It's normal to want to do things that we can be proud of. It's now becoming normal to intentionally be hard-done-by, struggling, and even destitute *as a point of pride.* Can you imagine what our ancestors, huddling in a cave, would think to see us cold or hungry, frustrated and unhappy, when the solution is so easily reached? We stubbornly choose to hold ourselves back to underline how we are right. We stubbornly live alone rather than having family around us.

Sometimes it starts when two people disagree about something. Rather than allow themselves to see the other person's point of view, maybe even allow it to change their minds, they become so attached to their opinion that their entire self-worth hinges on their rightness. It doesn't matter if that opinion is based on some scientific fact they heard about, or based on nothing at all.

When we attach ourselves to our opinion with such fervour and passion, we'll do anything to make sure it is never in question. We need to make sure our rightness never falters. We won't even consider simply agreeing to disagree. Somehow, we believe that the opinion we hold is a part of us, so if it were to be proven untrue, it would make us invalid—flawed deep down to our core—like we don't deserve to be here. Every argument is an attack on our very core identity, and to be wrong would mean becoming *no one.*

I've looked at this need to be right in myself, and here's how it seems to work for me. Deep down, my inner dialog says "if I were proven wrong now, what else have I been fooling myself about? Where else might I be wrong? How could all my beliefs be so messed up? How could *I* be so messed up? I wasted all those years believing something that isn't true!"

What if one belief you have had for a long time were not true? Would it actually be the end of you? What if something you frequently think about could be viewed differently? What if there were valid, excellent perspectives other than yours?

Can you imagine that nothing is black and white? Could you agree that there are things in the universe that can't be understood? Can you open your mind enough to say that there might be other perspectives that are valid? Are you willing to look at life from a slightly different perspective? Even if to do so is uncomfortable, can you be self-assured enough to consider trying a new perspective?

That is the place to start—to be willing to

Rightness Junkie

Psychologists have studied why we are so attached to our opinions, even when presented with scientific evidence that refutes them. They have found that we get a hit of dopamine when we encounter something that reinforces our beliefs, or when we have to defend our beliefs even if we are presented with evidence they are wrong. We also get a hit from winning an argument, which can cause fighting to become a real addiction for some.

see something differently—to see something with new eyes. It is empowering to look at the world with clear-headed openness to learning about it, and even allow something you learn to change you.

~

I love the idea of looking at myself as an anthropologist, a scientist studying me. I imagine that I am just here to learn about myself, here to see what's clunking around in that brain of mine, and see if any of it is illogical, ridiculous, or doesn't make sense with what I see in the world. Sometimes, I realize that I have been acting in ways that more-or-less guarantee failure and don't match up with what I see to be true, or what I feel is the way to thrive. When I pretend I'm an anthropologist, I can look at myself with a little detachment, a little scientific curiosity, rather than a sense that what I find out may be the end of me. Whatever I find will be interesting, and I can do what I like with that information. Even if it is surprising (shocking!) or uncomfortable, I still feel it is better to have information than ignorance. I'd like to learn what makes me tick, rather than just bumble along, wondering why I keep doing things to shoot myself in the foot, for example. This allows me to take a look at beliefs I have been holding and put them aside for a minute.

Conflict

When I argue with someone, I can't understand or rectify our two points of view. They are too different, and I label mine "right," of course, and the other person's "wrong." Sometimes, the two viewpoints are opposites, like two sides of a coin, but at other times, the two views may be on a spectrum, with a sliding scale between. In my mind, one end is "right" and the other "wrong."

Since it is so hard to admit I'm wrong, would it be easier to say that both of us are probably wrong? Often I argue adamantly about things that are very subjective, or things that I don't actually know that much about; but I am loathe to say I am not knowledgeable about a topic I've been talking about.

Giving up the need to be right may

require letting go of a love of conflict. Some see the world through the lens of conflict, and they get into a pattern of fighting with everyone. Behind most of the fights is a need to be right. Behind the need to be right is a deep insecurity.

The best way to begin is to set the intention to live more peacefully, even if you don't really know how. Decide that you want to step away from the pattern of fighting, from a life filled with conflict, and as you remind yourself of that decision daily, the way will become clear.

Acceptance

(The Cure for Frustration)

Do you know the creation story from Genesis? After God creates everything, there is a story of Adam and Eve and two trees. In this mythical story, the trees represent two options that Adam and Eve had to choose between. The trees were named *The Tree of Life* and the *Tree of the Knowledge of Good and Evil.*

The first tree's meaning is fairly obvious. Choose life. Choose to live, thrive, and be well. The second tree's meaning is more subtle. Many people misunderstand that second tree and believe that Adam and Eve had to choose between good and evil, but that's not the case. The tree is *called* the Tree of the *Knowledge* of Good and Evil.

Adam and Eve had to choose between being full of life **or** knowing/ judging good from evil. If they ate from the first tree, they would be childlike—lively, thriving, innocent—and if they ate from the second tree, they would be the judges of good versus evil, evaluators of what's right and wrong. They would lose their innocence and in the story in Genesis they suddenly know they are naked and they feel ashamed and try to hide from God.

Choosing the second option, to know the difference between good and evil, is choosing a life of frustration and death. The serpent in the story made it sound like it would be instant knowledge, but it isn't. We have to evaluate, label, and compare things to *decide in our own minds* if we deem them good or evil. **It is the attitude of judging and labeling that leads to death.** It's the death of our childlike spirit and freedom-loving vibe.

It's not our job to judge. What if they, and

we, walked away from needing to know what's right? What if we turned our backs on a belief in evil? What if we focused on simply living, instead of needing to know, judge, and label everything we come across? What if we decided not to wither and turn away from life?

This is our decision to make, as much as it was Adam and Eve's. We may choose life—a childlike trust that all is well—or we may choose the kind of thinking that leads to a premature death—critical, closed-minded, and labeling behaviour.

Choosing life means no more judging. It means accepting everything as good, or as simply true. There is no need to alienate anyone, to label them as evil. It means accepting the present situation without frustration. It means relaxing about our need to be perfect, and to have perfect surroundings.

When we learn to deeply accept the things and people around us, there is no foothold for frustration. There is no angst between what we feel is desirable and what is happening. We are simply in the moment, in the situation, with serene acceptance and grace.

For more on acceptance, see Tiny Book 1 *It All Belongs – The Law of Attraction and Nature of the Universe* and the chapter entitled "The Power of a Word: Acceptance."

Complementary Colours

There is a demonstration I used to do when I worked as an astronomer in a science centre to explain why the sky is blue. I filled a small aquarium with water and then added a little bit of milk to it. When white light is shone into the water, it looks bluish. When you put the aquarium onto an overhead projector and shine the light through it, the colour projected on the screen is orange, like a sunset. On a smaller scale, you can do this with a glass of water. Add a tiny bit of milk and it will look bluish. Shine a flashlight through the water onto a white wall and you will see orange light on the wall.

What is going on? The milk has done something to the water. It has added particles —impurities—that scatter the light. The colour blue is scattered most so that's what you see. Where did the red, yellow, or all the other colours go? They are being transmitted; they pass through the milky water just fine and come out the other side. That's why you see them projected onto the wall.

On a colour wheel, orange is the complimentary colour to blue, located on the opposite side of the colour wheel. Blue is a primary colour—it's not made up of any other colours—and orange is made up of the other two primary colours, red and yellow. Another way to think of it: if you mix blue and orange paint, you will get black. The same is true for the other complementary colours—if you mix yellow and purple paint, or red and green paint, you will get black.

I think this illustrates a point when it comes to "impurities" in our lives. When we want to change something about ourselves or our lives, we often try to apply the Law of Attraction with blunt force. For example, if we want to lose weight, we think that we need to focus on being thin. In general, we want to use the opposite of a problem as the problem's solution. We need less blue! What if we looked instead to its complementary colour, so to speak, and added more orange instead? Let me explain.

If wanting to lose weight is the problem, what does that really mean? Let's try to break the solution down into two other aspects, just as orange is comprised of red and yellow. We could think of being overweight as our bodies storing too much fat, and not burning enough fat. Most weight-loss programs do indeed tell us we must consume fewer calories and do more exercise. So, let's take a look at the complement of those issues. Storing too much fat or consuming too many calories is a bit like hoarding. It's the body holding on to reserves, "just in case." The complement to that is downsizing, decluttering, and not buying things we don't need. It is living leaner, not buying ridiculous amounts of things (shopping at bulk discount stores) and moving things out or getting rid of them when we no longer need them. Think about moving stagnant energy in our bodies and our homes. Could doing these things actually help us lose weight?

The second aspect is not burning enough fat, and many would agree this might relate to a slower metabolism or a lack of exercise. The complement here is taking correct action. Could my procrastination be the issue? Am I resisting doing something that I know deep in my heart I am supposed to be doing? This might be to forgive someone, apologize, or make amends. It could be many different things, and most likely, whatever pops into your head first is the issue at hand. So you can see, the solution to losing weight is not nearly as straightforward as you may think, and definitely not just about calories.

Let's look at another example. Suppose

the problem this time is not enough money. The two-fold solution that most people would say is to control expenses or increase income, right? Looking at the first one, controlling expenses, we might say we need to decrease the amount of money we are spending, because there just isn't enough. So, what is the complement to controlling expenses? Changing our belief that there isn't enough. We have to shift our belief in lack. This may not be a shock to you if you've been in new thought circles for a while, but it is a new way to come to that solution. It is leaving behind the teeth-clenching "how am I going to pay all these bills" paradigm for a more trusting, hopeful one.

Let's look at the second aspect, increasing income. Many would consider changing jobs, asking for a raise or taking on a second job. The complement to that is knowing that money can come from unusual places, and being alert to new opportunities. It is being as lighthearted as possible and willing to change one's attitude as well as do more or different work.

Here is one more example to help you see how complementary solutions work. Another common desire is for a new or better relationship. What are the two aspects to this? In essence, we don't like the person we are with and, more subtly, **we don't like who we are when we're with them.** Let that sink in for a minute.

~

What are the complements to these relationship issues? If we don't like the person we are with, we are obviously focusing on the things we don't like. We have to start looking for the good things about that person and focusing on those instead. Easier said than done at times, but it is essential.

The second aspect is equally important.

Sometimes, in certain circumstances or around particular people, we just don't like who we are becoming. It would seem we have to get away from those people, but this is not a real solution. What we must do to resolve this issue is reconnect with our true selves, act out of integrity, and **learn to like ourselves again.** As long as we are unhappy with who we are, we will be unhappy with anyone else.

We may be looking to relive that "summer of love" from our youth, but the key is that *back then, we thought we were awesome!* We had no hang-ups, and the boldness of youth made us think we were invincible as well. The realities of adult life may have squeezed those carefree, self-loving thought patterns out. It's no wonder we want to go back to being teenagers when we had few responsibilities and were masters of our domain! If your teenage years were full of strife, you may not relate to my analogy, but this applies to any time period that you have fond memories of. The reason we had such a great time in the past is that we *liked ourselves.* When we are able to learn to like ourselves, many other relationship issues resolve themselves. This solution may include the relationship ending—sometimes that has to happen when two people have grown too far apart.

This kind of thinking process can be applied to any problem. Pick two aspects of the problem and then ponder each one—or wait for an inspired message—until you get to the core of the issue. Ask "why?" until you are at the root, and then look for inspiration about what the complement to that issue is. Sometimes it is logical, like how needing more exercise equates to taking right action, and sometimes it is layered under false beliefs and unhealthy social norms. I met a young woman when I lived up north who became obese to discourage unwanted sexual attention. Her deep underlying belief was, "if I get big enough, they will leave me alone." Learning to deal with that unwanted attention, and be safe, is the real issue affecting many women's health. Obesity is actually a small aspect of what is going on.

Can you see how the real solution is not at all obvious sometimes? Don't rush the answers, and don't jump at the first shallow solution.

The complement can also be found by asking, "what feels more growth-oriented?" Often, one of the aspects will have a physical solution, like decluttering, and the other will involve an attitude shift. Taking physical action tells the universe—and yourself—that you mean business, but really shifting one's attitude is the most important part. It is best to shift your attitude first and then take action, but sometimes starting with a small action is a good way to start a shift.

Most important of all, be easy on yourself. This life is complicated; it's okay if it takes a little while to figure things out. Work on accepting yourself as fully as possible and be less judgmental of your own motives.

Heart Math

A long time ago I noticed that I get my best inspiration and coolest ideas just after I wake up. They float into my head, it seems—the elegant solution to a problem that I've been having, or an idea for a book, and so on. The ideas are often unexpected and the solutions not obvious. I never say to myself, "why didn't I think of this before?" because the new inspiration is usually very different from my normal way of operating. It's like I've been looking in the tall grass all over a field for the solution—my normal way of problem solving is to just keep doing what I'm doing *more*—and then I realize, "the grass *is* the solution!"

These inspirations are stunning and they used to be rare. I had paper by my bedside to write them down as soon as I could, in case I wouldn't remember them later. They were usually one sentence, like "the grass is the solution," and often changed my perspective greatly and suddenly. I noticed that the more I acted on them, the more they happened. And then I took a Heart Math class.

Heart Math uses slow, even breathing and putting your attention on the area of your heart to get your heart and brain into a harmonious state called coherence. The combination of focus and breathing is very easy and my life changed after I learned quick coherence—choosing to think about or relive a happy time or positive experience and therefore engage renewing emotions instead of depleting ones.

I took the class because I wanted to learn to listen to my heart more, and it definitely did that. One exercise we did, after we had been practicing for a few weeks, was to focus and breathe for a short time and then ask our heart for a solution to a problem we were having. My answer came almost immediately, and it was very profound. I realized that it was exactly like those messages, inspirations, and ideas that I got so rarely in those moments of waking up. It felt so incredible to tap into a source of wisdom and perspective as deep and wide as the ocean, any time I wanted, fully awake and alert.

A second exercise involved mind-mapping. Ordinarily, mind mapping is a style of brainstorming by jotting down aspects of a problem or project all over a piece of paper, connecting them in lines like a web. We did a normal mind map, and as usual, a torrent of words came out and I scribbled them down. After a few minutes, we were told to go into quick coherence and look at the paper again. New, thoughtful ideas came; they were better ways to think about the problem—ways that had the solution built in. They weren't clever. There wasn't a torrent of them. But they had heart.

In one class, our instructor, Luis, said that if you watch someone sleeping, their breathing is perfectly even. In a way, I'm in coherence whenever I sleep. In terms of biology, whenever I engage in even breathing —where the in-breath takes as long as the out-breath—I allow my body a time of rest. It feels like a waking nap; it is easier to rest my mind. I am not resisting the good that wants to come my way. The reason the profound ideas come at the moment of waking up is that I am still breathing evenly and in a state of freeflow from when I was asleep.

That must be why sleeping feels so good. We're in a state of non-resistance, where all our organs and cells are in harmony, communicating with each other freely. I use Heart Math to get to sleep more quickly. When I steady my breathing, slow it, and think about vaguely happy things, I can get to sleep very easily. I say "vaguely happy things" because I don't want to start engaging my imagination and my busy mind. I just want to float down a lazy river, happy and content.

I can now have a waking nap and feel renewed at times throughout my day. I can do it while I drive. I can do it at work, in between tasks. I can do it while I tidy up the house. I just have to remember that I have this tool in my toolbox! Most importantly, I can connect to the wisdom in my heart and hear its messages clearly. My head was so full of words and ideas, problems, and issues that my heart couldn't get through. I think my heart has been trying to help me for years—for my whole life?—and I haven't been paying attention. What if my body takes care of me instead of the other way around?

~

I used to think of my body as simply a container for the rest of me. Now, I believe it is much more profound than that. My physical body and I—my thoughts, consciousness, ego and personality—are an intimate partnership. We are joined. We are one. My brain is in charge, but I can choose to listen to the other members of the team—my heart, my gut, maybe even my legs—in the same way that I valued the experience and insight of my crew members on the York boat. If you haven't heard about my York boat expedition or read my book *York Boat Captain - 18 Life-Changing Days on the Peace River,* I'll summarize: I led a group of amazing individuals on a historical reenactment using a huge York boat on a river in the Canadian wilderness. It was an incredible experience of camaraderie, hard work, facing challenges together and learning to trust the river. I often asked my crew members for their input and suggestions; now I've also learned to ask my own heart.

A Sudden Impulse

of Self-Destruction

I don't know when the first one happened, but I have become consciously aware of short-but-intense bursts of self-loathing. Perhaps they started as a result of the abusive relationship I was in—that was the first time in my life I experienced hatred up-close-and-personal. Even though that was many years ago, there have been some definite side effects of that poison. However, I think these waves of emotion are unrelated. I realized recently that I used to vaguely dislike myself as a young adult and in university.

Sometimes, as the feeling of intense self-loathing comes on, I am able to remain conscious throughout the experience. When I say "remain conscious," I mean that I do not become so consumed by the feeling that I become associated with it—I feel the feeling but at the same time know it is not me. It's like the thoughts invaded my brain, as though I accidentally tuned in to a radio station. Sometimes, the hurtful thoughts come through clearly; other times it comes in feebly and garbled, but there is undoubtedly something being received.

The waves or bursts of self-loathing are very intense and rare, but I think that there is a fainter vibration of mild depression going on much more frequently. It is like:

- general dissatisfaction with aspects of my life
- feeling uncomfortable in my own skin
- disliking looking at myself in the mirror
- feeling frustrated with my surroundings

The bursts could be described as:
- intense self-hatred

- sudden desire to hurt myself
- suddenly wanting to sabotage my success
- irrational, consuming self-loathing

I struggle to put this into words in the hope that you can relate, so that you know you aren't alone. I know I might sound like a guru at times, but I have down days like anyone. Have you ever felt this way? Have you ever experienced these intense waves?

I certainly don't have all the answers, but I do have a few thoughts to share from my experiences. I have found that if I don't act on the intense emotion of self-hatred and simply endure it, it passes through me harmlessly. In fact, I had some insights into myself after they passed, so one might even say they were helpful. Thankfully, when they happened I was able to keep a small part of my consciousness apart from the emotion, which gave me a little space to observe what was happening. Even if you can only maintain a very small space, it is enough to help you not identify with the feeling as defining you. It may help to tell yourself, "something is happening to me. This is not me."

There is no point fighting it when it is happening or berating yourself afterwards. Neither of these activities helps you in the present, and the present is where you are now. It is the middle of the teeter-totter, the tipping point. *Now* is where we get to choose how to think, and decide if we will let something that happened in the past—even just moments ago—determine our future.

I like to think of the present moment as a thin slice of time. Imagine slicing an onion as thinly as you can. Then slice it even thinner, and thinner yet. The thinnest slice you can imagine is like the present moment. It is an instant in time, and even though it is thin, it packs a punch (like an onion). It contains all your decision-making power. Everything to come hinges on this moment. Will I be a kinder person? Will I thrive? Will I live lightly and easily? What direction am I going in?

Here's a little exercise for the next time you are meditating. Send your attention and energy away from your body, out into the universe. Then, bring it back again. Now, go inside, paying attention to your breath and heartbeat. Send your organs a little love. Now, bring your attention to your skin. That thin layer separating you from the universe is your skin; it is like the present moment. Away from your body is the future—doesn't it feel a bit like you are reaching for something you cannot know? Your internal body is the past— the health and state of your cells are a manifestation of how you've been treating yourself, but they are no indicator of the future. Your skin represents the present; bring your attention there to connect with the present moment.

Keeping your attention in the present moment is the key to having a tiny space to observe what is happening when overwhelming emotions come along. Practice when you feel good and you'll find it easier later, when you feel overwhelmed. Insights will follow; have a journal handy to jot them down. I discovered my pattern of doing little acts of self-sabotage—like not getting enough sleep—and then keeping the excuse handy so that if I failed, I was ready with my very reasonable story about why I couldn't be successful. And my story would not sound like self-sabotage, oh no. I had a bit of victim-thinking creeping in, long after I thought I had banished all that.

Gratitude

(The Cure for Self-Pity)

There are things to be learned by looking at the ugly sides of society and trying to understand what is going on at the deeper level. One of those ugly sides is domestic abuse. What causes one partner in a relationship to stop loving the other to such a degree that he/she starts abusing them? How could such a relationship go wrong?

Abusers are controlling, angry and threatening. They have volatile tempers and are extremely moody. They will even treat their victims good for a while and then unleash their controlling, violent behaviour again as part of a cruel cycle.

Abusers don't just act out because they

have issues with anger management, and *certainly* not because of something their victim did. They have much more dysfunction going on. They have very poor self-esteem, and they wrap themselves up in what I've come to realize is a very dangerous attitude: self-pity. They are very self-absorbed, and consumed with their own hardships. They are sometimes intensely self-critical and obsessed about their own (perceived) lack of success or status. They are jealous of everything good their partner has or does, and they feel threatened by anyone who is successful. They feel intensely sorry for themselves. They have excuses for why they aren't successful enough, why they don't get along with their boss or coworkers, and so on. When up close and personal, they are not loving or supportive of their mates whatsoever. They are more interested in keeping their partner in his/her place—squashing them down.

Domestic violence is an extreme case, but

it underlines how destructive self-pity is. Self-pity is pervasive in western society, and it has a thousand faces—it doesn't always result in abuse and isn't always as obvious as feeling sorry for oneself. We are indulging in self-pity whenever:

- we think we are hard-done-by
- we think that someone hasn't treated us fairly
- we complain about something we didn't get
- we complain that something didn't go our way
- we tell a story about why we are so unhappy
- we make excuses or invent self-justifying explanations in our heads
- we rehearse the reasons or story of why we are not successful
- we think we have it worse than anyone else and no one else could possibly understand.

All complaining is essentially a form of

self-pity, and complaining is a very popular activity! Self-pity can take you into a downward spiral, where you can't see the bottom nor imagine a way out. (It's a bit like depression in that way.)

I'll say it again—all complaining, excuses and many explanations are forms of self-pity. Feeling that you haven't been treated fairly is self-pity. Thinking that life is hard is self-pity. Most stories you tell yourself about how you ended up in this mess are self-pity. Self-pity leads to self-destruction, so be on the lookout for it and be ready to turn it around.

Thankfully, self-pity is one of the easiest attitudes to change. The cure for self-pity is **gratitude.** Self-pity fades in the presence of any sort of thankfulness or appreciation. You simply cannot be in a pity-party and grateful for life at the same time. Saying thank you as lip service will not do; it must be heartfelt gratitude. I'm so glad that many personal development gurus have encouraged us to foster an attitude of appreciation, and there are many great authors and speakers with ideas about how to live a life with more gratitude. Making a choice to be grateful, writing down things you are grateful for, and speaking about things you are thankful for are great ways to start! Focus on what you appreciate in life. Keep gratitude in the front of your mind and you will gradually weed out the self-pity. As a result, your quality of life and relationships will improve, and your overall happiness will multiply.

Holocaust survivors have said that the most important thing was not to feel sorry for yourself. Unbelievable. Take it from them and always be grateful.

Self-Acceptance

What if there was nothing wrong with you?

Let that sink in. There are a couple of different ways to take the meaning of that question. Let's look at those ways.

What if there was nothing wrong with you? What if you had the perfect health you have been asking for? What if you had the slim body you are after? What if you were happy, fulfilled, and living the kind of life you want? What if all your dreams came true in their entirety, right now, in this instant?

What next? Would you keep striving? Would you find something else to work on? If you were instantly slim, would you worry about the fat coming back? Would you start working on some other aspect of yourself? Or would you know how to relax in the new reality of nothing being wrong with you?

What if there was nothing wrong with you? What if you are great the way you are? What if thinking there is something wrong with you is just the most popular way to think about oneself, and it's so popular, no one really knows how to be content with who they are? What if being discontent sells more stuff at the drug store, and creates more trips to the mall for retail therapy? What if believing there is something wrong with you was just a simple belief, one that you can choose to no longer believe? When you were little, did you believe in Santa Claus, the tooth fairy or any number of other mythical beings? Beliefs can be changed.

What if you decided you didn't want to believe in illness anymore? It is very pervasive in our society. To believe that health is possible (even easy) is going against the grain.

What if you decided you didn't want to

believe there was anything wrong with your personhood—any profound reason you are single, or haven't gotten that new job you want, or found success in your new business endeavour, or whatever else you are working on? What if you are fine the way you are? What if you are more than fine? What if you are great? What if there is nothing wrong with you?!

The logical mind likes to look for answers to problems. Finding the answer to a problem is satisfying, don't you agree? So, it looks for problems. Why isn't my new business successful? Why can't I lose weight? It loves to look for reasons for things, to invent and speculate and even fabricate explanations. The ego jumps on board, too, since it loves to compare and criticize. We believe what we hear about the reason for this-or-that. These reasons and analyses easily become beliefs, as our mind convinces us that it has found the truth, however painful it may be.

What are some extreme cases of believing there is something wrong with you? One comes to mind—the breakup of a romantic relationship. Don't we immediately believe there must be something wrong with us? Don't we agonize over that? Don't we actually make the break-up worse the more we think along those lines?

Another example is anorexia. Young women (and men) can start to think they are fat and become so obsessed with their weight that all balance in their life is gone. They agonize and obsess over food. Their body image becomes completely distorted. Anyone looking at them sees they are skin and bones but they still think they are fat.

Could the same happen to us in other situations, such as after a relationship break-up? Could it be that we obsess over some aspect of ourselves to the point that we cannot see the truth anymore? We start to see ourselves as flawed, unlovable, or whatever other lies, in the same way the anorexic thinks she's fat. We aren't flawed or unlovable! We are just blind and hurting and our silly mind is looking for some reason to explain what happened. As the anorexic starves herself, so do we starve ourselves of self-acceptance and self-love.

~

What if there was nothing wrong with you? What if you decided to love and accept yourself just the way you are? When you think something is wrong with you it is the same as the anorexic believing she's fat. Your perspective is skewed; **there is nothing wrong with you,** you just think there is because it's what nearly everyone believes. Wouldn't you try to help an anorexic friend see that she is too thin? With the same fervour, try to help yourself see that there is nothing wrong with you.

Trust

(The Cure for Worry)

In the winter of 2009-2010, my husband and I started our own business, Flow North Paddling Company. We both loved to go canoeing and kayaking in the Canadian wilderness, so we decided to start a business so we could help others do the same. Although Darren helped, the canoe and kayak rental business that took shape was really my baby; I did the majority of the leg work to get the business going.

As anyone who's started a business knows, it was an enormous amount of work. I created a website, and found some canoes, kayaks and a canoe trailer to buy. On the advice of a lawyer, we decided to form a corporation. Finding insurance was a particular challenge, but after mentioning my struggles to several friends, I was referred to an excellent agent who became our insurance angel. There were a hundred details to take care of before paddling season began, and it was set to start with our first big event, Paddling the Peace, a one-day canoeing festival in the town of Peace River that I was asked to help with.

It was stressful, to say the least. I was still buying lifejackets just a couple of weeks before the event. There were paddles to label, rentals to arrange—every single one of our boats was spoken for—and to top it off, I was the person giving the safety briefings to all the participants while they rode the bus to the starting point. When the time came, the event went remarkably smoothly, with only minor logistics problems.

I should have felt relieved, and for about a day I did. But the stress that had been weighing me down for the last several months came back and I couldn't deny that I was worried.

This was our business. We needed this income. This was a big endeavour and it just had to be successful.

I continued with this attitude for most of our first summer. I found relief from the worry occasionally, when I was really having fun out on the water, but it was never very far from me.

In October, Darren and I attended a business development seminar presented by Donald Cooper, former owner of Cooper Canada, one of the premier sporting goods manufacturers in North America, and very successful businessman. He taught us many principles of management and marketing and generously shared his wisdom with us. One thing that he said really struck me at the time: trust the process. Once we have done what needs to be done—followed his methods and taken all the right steps—we need to *trust* that the process will work.

Many months later the fundamental truth crystallized for me: **trust is the cure for worry.**

We all worry. From the moment we become adults—perhaps worrying is even the defining moment of adulthood—we are all susceptible to worry. Young children don't worry; they have "the trust of a child." To be free from worry is to be more child-like, and to be more child-like is to leave stress behind —to play more and thrive more.

Use Your Imagination for Good

What is worrying, exactly? Worrying is a negative pattern of imagining the worst outcomes.

As with so many of our common struggles, worrying is all in our heads. Certain external stimuli, like the news or people around us, might start the worry ball rolling, but it's our thoughts and *our imagination* that keep it going.

Our minds are the places of secrets—secret dreams and secret fears. In the realm of the imagination, anything is possible. We imagine how we'll respond to the challenges we face, and whether they will be easy or hard. Infinite joys and innumerable sorrows can take place exclusively between our ears, never see the light of day, and yet they thrill or torment us like the cold hard metal of reality. Imagination is a blessing, yet it can seem like a curse when it takes us down a dark path of frightening events and bad outcomes.

Yet we are not slaves to our imagination. Just as we can choose to have conscious control of what we think, we can decide what path our imagination will follow. We can learn to use our imagination for good and overcome the tendency to worry.

We have to practice staying in the present moment, otherwise we risk being swept away into the past or the future—both states are fueled by our imagination. Whenever you realize you've been worrying, snap yourself back to this exact place and time. Take a deep breath and soften your facial expression. Let some of your tension melt away.

It takes some practice, but you can learn to catch your imagination as it goes down a worrisome path and change the direction before you have spun an elaborate negative story. You can learn to do Heart Math to calm yourself down and increase your resilience.

Using your imagination for good is only a tool, however. The cure is learning to trust.

Do you remember playing the trust game when you were young, where your friend stands behind you and you fall back and let her catch you? Each time, she steps farther away, and you fall farther, nearly to the ground before being caught. It's a game of trust, and it always got my heart pounding. To play the game right, you are supposed to keep falling back while your friend catches you, over and over again, to see how much you trust her. Was I the only one who, the whole while, was struggling to trust?

The problem I had with any of my friends, as much as I liked them, was I just couldn't trust that they wouldn't drop me. I mean, they were kids just like me—how did I know they wouldn't make a mistake and drop me? Rather than trusting, I worried, the opposite of what I was supposed to be doing!

Trust is the cure for worry on the vibrational level. To cure the biggest worries, you'll need to truly, deeply trust in something bigger than yourself. This is the fundamental principle, and you can decide what you want to trust in; it doesn't really matter what you choose, as long as it is real and deep to you. Let's explore this further.

Trusting God

"God" is such a big word, and it has so many different meanings for people. I will borrow a principle from Alcoholics Anonymous and say that the best thing to do is trust in God "as you understand him to be." In this section, I will speak of God as most Christians do.

There are many aspects to trusting God, but here are a few to think about:

- trust that God is real, powerful, and personal
- trust that God hears your prayers
- trust that God will take care of you and all your needs will be provided for
- trust that you are forgiven and there is no harsh judgment waiting for you.

Depending on what you worry about most, you can tailor a devotion or affirmation that will help you develop more trust. If you worry a lot about money, find passages that promise God will provide. He does not want you to worry! Write the scriptures that speak to you the most on cue cards or make signs to put up on your mirror or fridge. Memorize a few to use throughout your day. The more often you remind yourself of your beliefs and reassure yourself, the easier it will be to trust and you will find your worry gradually evaporates.

Trusting Source

Perhaps your perspective of God is less personified than the Bible, and you'd rather think of God as *Source*, the *Universe*, *All-That-Is* or *the Vortex*. Again, it's a matter of different words or perspectives, but let's continue along this line.

What are your beliefs about Source? Do you believe you are here to thrive? What kind of universe do you feel you live in? Some thoughts that might help you develop more trust are:

- trust that everything is good and perfect in your life
- trust that you are here to thrive
- trust that you are here to grow, and growth does not have to be painful or difficult
- trust that you always have access to the support and inspiration you need
- trust that your intuition will guide you to take the best course of action

Whatever you believe, there *must* be an aspect of trust in it. Find that aspect and meditate on it, focus on it, and make it more real in your life. Build up your trust until it is a strong feeling that you can recall and go back to often throughout your day, preventing worry from cropping up.

The Laws of Physics

Atheists worry too, and the cure for worry will absolutely work as well for you as for those with religious beliefs. If you have a hard time believing in God, you can choose to believe and trust in something else, deeply and personally, to cure your worry. One example is the laws of physics.

When I refer to the Laws of Physics, I am generalizing to include all sciences. Physics is constant and does not waver, and in many ways can be more comforting and real than invisible deities. But how will trusting in physics help you not to worry?

Physical principles can be generalized and applied to everyday life. For example, take work. Work is force times distance. In life, this means that if you put in some effort (force) and keep at it (go the distance), success is inevitable (work will occur). Focusing on this principle can help you not to worry whether your work will pay off—*trust* that it will, because physics says it will. Trust the process.

Here is another one, using logic: if time is money, and if money is power, then time is power (influence). If you give someone your time, you will have more influence in their life. Your relationship will be stronger. If you have been worrying about your relationship with someone, try giving them more time and then trust that your relationship will improve.

Other ways to trust in physics:

- trust that you can remain grounded in stressful times (just as gravity always works on an object's center of mass)
- trust that your efforts for clear communication will be successful (the signal will get through)
- trust that your hard work will pay off
- trust that the seed that is planted and tended will grow
- trust that if you feed your body healthy foods it will grow healthy cells.

Remember, the goal is to keep enough of the essence of *trust* in your mind to leave no room for worry—to keep the "kryptonite" active. Obviously, the above points work for non-atheists equally well!

The Law of Attraction

The Law of Attraction states that similar things attract each other, and it operates much like a law of physics; you don't have to know anything about it for it to still operate. It is universal and acts on everyone the same. It is always working, consistently and continually, and you instinctually understand how it works (as a child understands gravity without knowing a single equation).

- trust that the Law of Attraction is always at work
- trust that you *can* orchestrate your life
- trust that what you are manifesting is coming soon
- trust that changing your life can be relatively easy once you change your attitudes.

See Tiny Book #1 *It All Belongs – The Law of*

Attraction and Nature of the Universe for more about the Law of Attraction.

The Essence of Trust and Worry

Try this exercise: get on a train of thought that inspires you to trust, and ride it for a while until you are really feeling good. Just keep thinking thoughts that help you to feel trust, and combine it with the free feelings of a child, until you are flying high emotionally. Breathe deeply and become aware of how that feels in your body. Now, for just a split second, think whatever thoughts normally cause you to worry. Did you feel something change? Can you feel a distinct "flip-flopping" inside? Quickly reestablish the trusting thoughts so that you don't get into a spiral of worry. Breathe deeply a few times.

Isn't it surprising how quickly your vibration can change? It is amazing how strongly those entrained thoughts—the ones we practice frequently without meaning to—

can set up a chain reaction of emotion. The good news is, you can train yourself to feel better by setting up strong feelings of well-being and then when you want to feel better, you can think certain "trigger thoughts" and go to a better-feeling place as quickly as you were previously going downhill.

When you are feeling really good, try to identify what types of thoughts got you to that place. Was it music you love, or were you focusing on something you love to do, like a hobby or recreational activity? Were you thinking of how many neat advances our society has made? Or were you just driving with the top down, enjoying the sun? What thoughts led to you feeling so good?

I can *guarantee* you weren't listening to the news! I highly recommend reducing or removing the amount of news you take in throughout the day while you work on happy-thought-entrainment. In fact, I hardly ever watch or read the news, and I am much happier without it. Not listening to the news does not make you a bad person, and it *will* make you much happier and improve your focus on all that's good in this world.

Consider a bad-news story about serious forest fires in Russia. Unless you live in eastern Europe, this news item does not actually affect you, but it may set up a series of worrisome thoughts. **When you have no intention of helping in a situation, bad news is not helpful to you in any way.** Censoring or limiting news is a very simple, practical thing you can do to very quickly reduce your worry. It is a bit like a smoker who is trying to quit avoiding all the usual trigger situations— coffee breaks or eating lunch on a restaurant patio. Avoid the worry-trigger of the news until you can feel empathy without worry. Whenever you do watch, practice imagining the best for the people on the news.

I love applying "muscle" from an area I am strong to an area where I am weaker.

Would it be helpful to go to a swimming pool, float in the water and trust it to hold you up, and just soak up that *trustingness*? It would work as long as you aren't terrified of water!

It's as simple as this: worry spirals around a myriad of bad things that *could* happen; trust says that nothing bad is going to happen.

Integrity

(The Cure for Anxiety)

Remember the snowstorm from chapter one? Often when I'm driving and it starts to snow, I wonder if it is actually starting to snow everywhere, or am I just driving into an area where it's coming down. It is impossible to tell. I start wondering if it is snowing to the same degree at home. Or am I headed into an area of worse snow?

As long as I keep moving, there is no way to know if the increase in snow is due to my motion—driving into an area of snow—or due to time—the snow starting everywhere. The only way to know is to stop moving as soon as I see the first flakes. Then, if the snow is increasing, I can be fairly sure that it's starting everywhere. If it isn't, then I must be entering a localized area of snow. It works exactly the same with rain.

But I don't stop. I always keep going. If it starts coming down really thick, I tend to worry about how bad the roads will be. (Then I have to practice trusting!)

Snowy roads are just one of a thousand things that can cause anxiety, and the key is to stop what I'm doing. I need to pause and look around—watch the snow falling, so to speak—and see what's going on.

Could my intuition be trying to tell me something? If I am hell-bent on continuing, I won't listen. Often, I have some totally arbitrary goal in mind that I could easily change or even decide to abandon, but as long as I'm moving, I can't seem to do it. When I stop my frantic action, I can stop my momentum and reassess what I've been doing. For example, is rushing from place to place to buy Christmas presents for distant relatives really necessary? Why am I so anxious? When I stop, I remember that I don't actually believe in buying Christmas presents for distant relatives (close relatives are enough). So I'm acting against my beliefs, and my intuition has been trying to remind me of that. When I'm in the middle of my day, in the throes of busyness, my intuition has limited messages it can get through to me. Sending a feeling of anxiety is supposed to work. It's supposed to feel so bad, I have to stop, take a few deep breaths and figure out what's causing the anxious feeling. From a Heart Math perspective, my thoughts make my breathing erratic, which makes my heart beat irregularly, and so I feel anxious.

Unfortunately, many of us have become so accustomed to living with anxiety, we don't ever stop and listen to what is causing it. We live with so little mindfulness and so much contradiction in our lives. For example, we want to decrease the gap between the rich and the poor, yet we shop at places owned by—give our money to—the richest. We want politicians who listen, yet we don't actually take the time to tell them what we are upset about. We complain about things but don't take a single small step to make a change. We could go to that locally-owned cafe for lunch. We could send our elected representative an email, or join a movement for positive change. We could really look at what we believe and what kind of world we want to live in, and then **do things to support that vision**—acting with integrity, mindfully. We could do less overall, and make what we do really count.

~

Most importantly, remind yourself that

Integrity: The only person you really have to live with is yourself. When you do your best to act with integrity—according to your beliefs—then your inner environment has less conflict and anxiety fades.

small things that seem to threaten us so greatly have no real ability to impact our deeper lives, our eternal nature. No amount of *anything* can touch who we really are. We are here to have these experiences because they are glorious and thrilling. Yes, they are challenging, but only because we are so capable.

Slow down and think. Stop altogether so your intuition, your heart, can get its real message through. Take action accordingly—which may be no action at all, or it may change everything about how you live.

Remembering Stella

Some days, you just have to do the thing you don't want to do.

Death makes you face things and do things that you just don't want to. You can't leave it until later. You can't deny it. You have to find some strength within—and you always do—to be able to do what you must. In my case, that was take care of our sweet, fluffy barn kitty who passed away unexpectedly.

Her name was Stella. I gave her that name one cool, autumn day, after moving back to the farm I grew up on. She was a little black and white cat who lived in the hayloft of the barn. We'd see her sitting out on the edge, catching some sun on cool October days, but if we approached the barn too purposefully, she'd be off like a flash, into a hidden part of the hayloft. She was so skittish!

We would climb the ladder to feed her every day, and at first, she was barely visible, peeking out from a hidden part of the hayloft. Before too long, though, she became a little more exposed, a little closer, and one of my favourite memories of her was the time she came to the food bowl before I had even gone down two rungs of the ladder—I got to see her up close for once! She was so sweet! Most of the time, though, she would sit on a nearby disintegrating bale of straw and look at us. The look on her face said, "you're going to feed me again? Why are you being so nice to me?" It was sad that she was so baffled by our care and interest in her. For the last couple of months, however, she no longer had the look of confusion on her face. She was still cautious, though—as she approached so much of her life, I suppose. She understood that we would bring her food every day and that we loved her. At least I hope she understood that last part.

One wintry day, Darren found her unmoving in the hayloft. He had gone to give her fresh water, and he didn't see her at first. Then he saw her, laying with her chin on the straw, not moving. When I got home, he told me that we'd lost her, so I went straight to the barn. I saw her as I climbed the ladder. It seemed strange—I had never seen her in that part of the hayloft before. But we knew her so little! We only saw her for a few minutes a day. What was her life really like? We have no way of knowing. We only know that she had lost the tips of her ears to frostbite over harsh winters of the past. We know she had at least one litter of kittens—my mom had told us that, and that's the only way they'd known she was a she. You just couldn't get close enough to her.

Was she ever mistreated? I don't think so. She simply is—ahem, was—a barn cat. She caught mice, and maybe birds, as her main diet. Yet her look improved greatly once we started feeding her regularly. Her coat got fluffier, she seemed to put on some weight, and she looked less scared. I don't think she was ever mistreated before; it's just the way of a barn kitty. She got table scraps sporadically, and other than that, she was independent. She lived out there, and we live in the house, and we just didn't know her very well.

The first time I got to pet her was after she'd died. Despite all I just said about barn cats, I feel it is a shame I never got to connect with her, pet her and show her more affection while she was alive. She was so soft, and so sweet, and still warm! It seemed like she had just stopped breathing, and she might start up again any second. What would she do? Would she try to bolt away, suddenly aware that she had let her guard down too much? Or would she sigh and purr and then die again, but this time, knowing for sure that she was loved?

~

I chose a bright yellow piece of cloth to wrap her in. It seemed the most appropriate for her, but my mood was anything but sunny. I didn't want to do it. I didn't want to have to take care of her body. I wanted her to be alive; I didn't want to be in this situation. Then, quite out of the blue, I thought, *every day, we have new opportunities. And today, this is my opportunity.* What a strange thought to come to me, and it vastly changed my perspective. It's my opportunity to take care of the body of my sweet kitty. Not an obligation, or unpleasant task. It's my chance, and it only comes once.

I cried quite a bit, still caught up in the "what ifs" and "if onlys." But, like so many facing death, I consoled myself with "we did our bests" and "I think she loved us." It's all we can do, with so many unknowns.

~

How do we get through a time of grief? Is

it okay to console ourselves rather than wallowing in sorrow? I think so. After Stella passed away, I gave myself permission to console myself whenever I needed it, using whatever means necessary. I cannot bear falling into a bottomless pit of sorrow. If a simple thought, however trite, helps me feel better, I use it. In a time like this, there's always the temptation to live in the past and/ or feel sorry for myself, but if I focus on things to be grateful for, I can avoid that.

So let this be my tribute to you, dear Stella. I have the feeling you enjoyed your time on this earth. I hope you know how much you meant to us. This isn't the last time we'll think of you! We'll miss seeing you in the hayloft every day. Thank you for the opportunity to care for you. Although you are gone, we won't forget you.

Humility as a Source of Joy

I remember the first time I really listened to a bird's song and wondered what it was singing. I was laying on my back in a tiny blue tent, somewhere on the bank of the Peace River, in the middle of a multi-day solo kayak trip. I had just woken up and a bird nearby—I didn't know what kind—was singing its song loudly and regularly. I heard it sing its musical phrase, repeating itself over and over but changing the tune slightly each time. As I listened, I realized that during the pauses, another bird far off in the distance was answering it. They were singing back and forth to each other. I wondered what they were saying. I imagined that the near one was saying, "it's still here. The big blue thing is still here. [pause] Yes, it's still here. The big blue tent thing is still just sitting here..." The far one was asking each time, "is it still there? Is the weird blue thing still there?" I realize it's a little ego-centric to assume they were talking about me, but I am fairly certain they had never seen a blue tent before.

Another time, more recently, I was relaxing in our hammock and gazing up at the two trees that were holding me up. A bird landed way up in the top of one of the trees and started singing. Its song also repeated with a few small variations. I tried to see it, but there were too many leaves, so I just enjoyed the sound and sunshine. I was in an interesting head-space and wasn't really thinking about much when it hit me: the bird was singing, "it's all good up here. Everything looks good to me!" and that's what birds sing ninety-nine percent of the time. The only time they aren't singing that song is when they are making an alarm call to warn their mate or neighbour of danger.

Birds, and all of nature, are holding the high watch all the time. Are you familiar with this phrase, "hold the high watch?" It is similar to raising the vibration or when lightworkers say they are holding the space. To me, holding the high watch means you're seeing the best in the situation, or believing in a good outcome. Although it is a great idea and does make a difference in a room, it is not necessary. All of nature is doing that all the time. It sings to the Universe, continually, "it's all good over here! Everything is good!" I wonder if the different bird songs are just different ways of saying that. "Everything is perfect here! Perfect here" or perhaps, "what a beautiful world, beautiful!"

Lightworkers, those seeking enlightenment, and you, reading this book, are not immune to thinking that we need to raise the vibration of this-or-that *as a form of pride.* We think we need to be there, to "tap in," meditate, harness crystals, or any number of other things. We don't. Nature is vibrating at the highest level all the time. It works together harmoniously for all to succeed. I believe that the cure for every illness is in a plant somewhere on this planet! There are multiple cures, in fact; for example, plantain is good for itchy skin, but so are tea tree, lavender, and juniper berries.

I went out to pick wild rose petals one hot, breezy day. They were in full bloom, the bees were buzzing around them, and the grass was high among them. They were so gorgeous and abundant, perfect and aromatic. I knew they held healing properties I needed—that the world needed. So I was there to gently pick some of their petals to partake, to share, in their beauty and perfection. I didn't disturb any flowers that had bees, flies or ants in them. It is difficult to describe, but as I slowly and gently picked the petals, I was humbled. These roses, covering a small hill on our land, were so giving, gorgeous, and utterly humble.

As I picked the petals, I was in awe and also humbled.

Humility gives me insight, clarity and peace. It disempowers my ego. I can see the truth of situations that I cannot see when I'm blinded by pride. The analogy is a good one—pride blinds you not only to your own flaws, but also to the truth of a situation, the beauty in another, and the possibilities that are out there.

I've known for a while that being in nature is the easiest way for me to find peace and clarity, and that sense is most profound when I am humbled. Have you ever been to a forest of redwoods, huge cedars or pines? It's humbling. However, sometimes when I go walking on a nature trail I forget to appreciate the greater Intelligence—I could be distracted by a thousand thoughts whirling through my head. But when I look around and remember the awe and miracle of it all, I am humbled, and that is when I am my best self.

Humility is a super-power. It gives me insight and wisdom. It clears my vision, so clouded by pride and ego. The Universe does not need me to raise its vibration. I don't need to meditate more for the sake of the physical planet. I don't need to do anything! The world of nature is already vibrating incredibly high, and nothing mere humans do changes that. When we work to raise the high vibration of the world, whatever we do is like a drop in the ocean. Every drop adds up, just do not become prideful in your lightwork or meditation. Activists and lightworkers can be full of ego and pride, just like anyone else.

When we hold the high watch, we change ourselves and those around us. We change our vibration and perspective and that changes how we see the world and what we manifest. When we are really clear, we can tap into the Universal Mind and affect the outcomes of things immediately around us, and I've found there's a matter-of-fact-ness about the best practitioners, not pride.

Remember the redwoods before you try to raise the vibration in a room. Once a year, when they bloom, sit with the wild roses and be in awe of their healing properties. We are so blessed to be here, in every moment. Be humbled often, and be lighthearted and you will tap into a sweet, gentle, and resilient joy that is everywhere present.

Teresa Griffith

Be Happy No Matter What

(The Cure for Complaining)

Remember the two trees from chapter four? One was the tree of life and one was the tree where you judge, evaluate and determine what's right and wrong. One is the way of the heart, and in the other, the head prevails. One is innocence and thriving, and the other is aging and shrinking.

Never forget you get to choose what tree to go sit under. You can choose to go towards Life at any time. In every moment, that choice is yours.

It is possible to have sustainable happiness, a thriving, adventurous life, harmonious relationships, and ease in all aspects of your life if you decide that your happiness matters. Choose Life. Choose to stop judging and be happy no matter what.

Sound impossible? Unrealistic? Make sure you read all the way to the end of this chapter. It's the most important attitude of all—that's why I've saved it for last. The biggest roadblock to choosing happiness is also an obvious one: complaining. Many people have made it a hobby—even a full-time job!—to judge and complain about everything they encounter. Most complaining comes from self-pity, and we've already talked about how destructive that is.

To experience sustainable wellness you simply must stop complaining. You must bite your tongue on it. You must not let a whiny word past your lips. It will not be easy.

When my husband and I were first together, I noticed something alarming about his behaviour. He liked to complain about all kinds of things. I had been living a pretty content life, so when he joined me, his complaining was jarring.

Within weeks of him moving in, I started pointing out whenever he complained about something. Rather than nag with words, I would poke him in the side—I'm not sure it was kinder than words, but it worked for us! Before long, I could make the motion from across the room and he realized that he'd done it again. He became very aware—acutely aware—of when he was complaining, and he learned to cut it short.

In fact, within a year, he stopped complaining altogether. If he did, he kept it all inside for fear of being poked! I'm certain that our relationship would not be as lovely as it is now if he had continued his pattern of complaining. Don't you agree how annoying it is listening to someone complain?!

When you complain, you are saying to the universe, "nothing here is good enough for me," when in fact the opposite is true. Everything is perfect as it is. Your judgment of the situation only showcases your ignorance of the depth and breadth of what is truly going on. Forces of the universe came together to create your world—a perfect incubator for your growth. Through sublime and mysterious variations of your vibration, you have asked for this precise experience.

So, you simply must. Stop. Complaining. In any way you can. You must realize that nothing is more important than your happiness—not being right, not being informed, not being comfortable, not anything. It is so important that you find a way to tap into the deep, incredible well of *wellness.* Complaining takes away your ability to see the well, never mind tap in. Your mental and physical health depend on you putting a priority on it. Nothing is more important than choosing happiness, choosing life.

Decide that you won't let any situation steal your happiness—whether it's a traffic jam, messy kids, bills to pay, world events, or any other situation that arises. You can be happy in anything. People who have contracted terminal illnesses report feeling happy. Their lives come into focus and they don't complain about the myriad of mundane things we complain about on a daily basis. Some of the poorest people on the planet are also some of the happiest. Anyone in any situation can be happy, if they do not complain. There are always things to be grateful for; why not talk about those things instead of complaining?

You can allow happiness to be the overarching theme of your life. Sometimes, I am achy, but I'm achy-and-happy. I have been tired-but-happy, busy-but-happy, flustered-but-happy and so on. The happiness prevails throughout, whenever I am conscious enough to remember that I have decided, definitely, absolutely, to be happy no matter what.

There is nowhere else I'd rather be! This is where all the good stuff is. This is where life is interesting and fulfilling! Being happy is easy when I am mindful of what tree I am sitting under.

~

Decide that your internal happiness matters more than ever, and it doesn't depend on circumstances. If something in life is making it very difficult to be happy, change what you must to move to a better-feeling place. Quit that awful job, or carefully extract yourself from that belittling relationship. I'm not saying cover the crapola in your life with affirmations and platitudes until you are fake-happy. I'm saying choose the path of true happiness, even if it is going to be a bit awkward and uncomfortable for a little while. You can be uncomfortable-but-happy in the meantime. If wellness is your desire, go after it, and don't let anything you might feel like complaining about stand in your way. **Stop complaining and be grateful, or change your situation.**

You are in charge of your life—no one else.

Decide what tree to sit under, and go sit under it. Stubbornly. Happily! Even if you are the only person you know thriving, do it. You will meet the rest of us under there, hanging out and napping in the shade of the Tree of Life.

Two Trees

Appendix

Chart Relating Attitudes to Chakras

I'm including this chart if you would like to research how to strengthen one of the chakras relating to a particular attitude.

The cure for:	is:	related to the:
Anxiety	Integrity	red (1st) chakra
Worry	Trust	orange (2nd)
Frustration	Acceptance	yellow (3rd)
Self-Pity	Gratitude	green (4th)
Being Right	Willingness	blue (5th)
Self-loathing	Self-acceptance	indigo (6th)
Complaining	Decide to be Happy	purple-white (7th)

Two Trees

About the Author

Teresa Griffith draws inspiration from nature and shares stories from her life on a small farm in Canada. She has also written *Love Your Skeletons,* a guide to overcoming painful or embarrassing skeletons in your closet, and *York Boat Captain -- 18 Life-Changing Days on the Peace River.*

In her series of Tiny Books on Big Ideas, she shares revolutionary principles and observations of how the universe works, the roots of happiness, connecting with profound intelligence, and deep, inspired wisdom on relationships with others and ourselves.

For more information or to contact Teresa, visit teresagriffith.ca.

Two Trees

www.ingramcontent.com/pod-product-compliance
Lightning Source LLC
LaVergne TN
LVHW021549080426
835510LV00019B/2449